Khloe's Beautiful Blues is dedicated to Lucy. I hope this reminds you and other girls whose skin was kissed by the sun that you are beautiful. You are an original design. You are a perfect work of art.

Published by Orange Hat Publishing 2022
ISBN 9781645388913

www.orangehatpublishing.com

Foreword

Who would have the prolific capacity to take emotions of dejection, coupled with a term of endearment, thereby creating an oxymoron to shed a glaring light of encouragement to the souls of the reader? In other words, how could "blues" be beautiful? It is of no surprise that through this piece, author La'Ketta Caldwell has found a way to express such feelings. *Khloe's Beautiful Blues* addresses the epidemic of childhood bullying through poetry. Its intent is to encourage those of minority background to be courageous and confident in who they are.

La'Ketta strongly believes that the youth should have a voice; her day-to-day work and philanthropic efforts speak to her beliefs surrounding the upbuilding and nurturing of the youth. The poetic justice of this book reminds children of the beauty that lies within our differences. Amidst our ethnic backgrounds and within the depths of our skin tone lies a rich heritage full of magnificence, wisdom, legacy, and strength. As La'Ketta expresses: "This sonnet is dedicated to young women whose skin was kissed by the sun."

I have had the distinct pleasure of watching a poetic dream of creative arts come to fruition through La'Ketta's vast work across plays, short skits, musicals, and social movements. La'Ketta's expressions in this book reinforce the reader to think of the context of beauty that can only be created by a higher being, and that should be internally revered, yet not often externally accepted.

Quite often, beauty has been defined by the world through skin tone and measurements. It has only been within the past few years that beauty has been accepted by people to encompass those from all social classes. And while this is true from media and modeling industries to embrace all, one would hope that the same or perhaps even a stronger message would begin to trickle down to those who are the most impressionable, who grow up to either be driven by beauty or purpose.

Now that we are exposed to *Khloe's Beautiful Blues*, it is my sincerest desire that real discussions take place where it matters most, where the bullying ends and the acceptance begins: in the hearts and minds of the youth.

Kimberly R. Lock
speaker, author, publisher, philanthropist

Beautiful Blues,
Beautiful Blues,

Hues deeply covering skin.

Your beauty glows,
And it shows

Your
royalty within.

Across the waters,
Across the seas,
Your reflection is a reminder
Of our *history.*

Beautiful Blues,
Beautiful Blues,

Dry your weeping eyes.

Not surprised
others can't see the

prize.

Stand up straight,
Block out the noise that destroys.

Your beauty spreads on the outside
And flows from within your *heart.*

The music of your heartbeat,
The rhythm of your hips,

The history in your veins,
Treasure *flows* from your lips.

Beautiful Blues,
Beautiful Blues,
Loving *smile* and
Contagious *laugh,*

I cannot help but
Speak *life*
on your
behalf.

Beautiful and smart,
The sound of your essence
Creates a *groove.*

We tap our feet and move
To the beat
of your
heart.

Beautiful Blues,
    Beautiful Blues,

Your song is
**one of
a kind.**

Dry your weeping eyes,
The world just may not see
The essence
of your
beauty.

That does not mean it is not true.

If no one ever told you,
You're enough just the way you are.

The sun knew you were special
And kissed you from afar.

Beautiful Blues,
Beautiful Blues,

CPSIA information can be obtained
at www.ICGtesting.com
Printed in the USA
LVHW070844210722
723997LV00015B/426